D1141080

521 700 54 7

I ♥ Craft

PAINTING
and
DRAWING

Rita Storey

W
FRANKLIN WATTS
LONDON • SYDNEY

First published in 2015 by
Franklin Watts
338 Euston Road
London NW1 3BH

Franklin Watts Australia
Level 17/207 Kent Street
Sydney NSW 2000

Copyright © Franklin Watts 2015
All rights reserved.

Packaged for Franklin Watts by Storeybooks
rita@storeybooks.co.uk
Designer: Rita Storey
Editor: Sarah Ridley
Crafts made by: Rita Storey
Series editor: Sarah Peutrill
Photography: Tudor Photography, Banbury
www.tudorphotography.co.uk

A CIP catalogue record for this book is available
from the British Library.

Printed in China

Dewey classification: 745.5'941

ISBN (hardback): 978 1 4451 3082 8
ISBN (library ebook): 978 1 4451 3083 5

Cover images: Tudor Photography, Banbury

Franklin Watts is a division of Hachette Children's Books,
an Hachette UK company
www.hachette.co.uk

Before you start

Some of the projects in this book require scissors, glue,
a microwave oven, acrylic paint and sharp objects. When using
these things we would recommend that children are supervised
by a responsible adult.
Please note: keep home-made products
away from babies and small children.
They cannot be tested for safety.

Contents

Doodle Bookmark

Doodles are random shapes and patterns. People sometimes make designs called 'doodles' when they are on the telephone or thinking about something else.

1 Using the black felt-tip pen, doodle some shapes on one piece of card. Copy the pattern shown above or make up your own.

You will need:

* fine point black felt-tip pen

* 2 pieces of thin white card, 50mm x 210mm

* fine point red felt-tip pen

* fine point green felt-tip pen

* 10cm length of thin ribbon

* PVA glue and spreader

You can use coloured ballpoint pens instead of felt-tip pens.

2 Draw smaller shapes inside each large shape.

3 Fill in the spaces between each shape with lines or patterns, as shown.

4 Use the black felt-tip pen to make some of the lines thicker.

5 Draw patterns between some of the lines using the red felt-tip pen.

6 Use the green felt-tip pen to fill in more areas and complete the design. Repeat steps 1 – 6 to decorate the other piece of card.

7 Lay one of the pieces of card with the decorated side face down. Spread the card with glue. Fold the ribbon in half and place the doubled over ends at one end. Spread some more glue over the ribbon as shown.

8 Press the undecorated side of the second piece of card onto the glue with the ribbon sandwiched in between. Leave to dry.

Leave the bookmark between the pages of a book to mark your place.

Frog Flip Book

Flip the pages and watch this hungry frog catch his lunch!

You will need:

* a small pad of sticky notes (or staple some squares of coloured paper together)

* black felt-tip pen

You could hold the paper up to a bright window to help you trace the picture.

1 Use the felt-tip pen to draw a frog on the lower half of the last sticky note in the pad. Copy the frog on page 32 or make up your own.

2 Working from the back, flip down the next sticky note. Trace the frog through the paper, onto this sticky note. Draw a fly to the left of the frog.

3 Repeat step 2 and add the tip of the frog's tongue, sticking out of its mouth.

4 Repeat step 2 several times. Every time you draw the frog, show its tongue getting longer and nearer to the fly.

5 Draw the frog's tongue touching the fly.

6 In the next picture, draw the frog's mouth closed and leave the fly out of the picture.

7 Draw a few more pictures with the corners of the frog's mouth curling up into a smile.

8 Take hold of the pad with your fingers on the top and your thumb at the bottom. Lift the pages up.

9 Let the pages go, one at a time, so that you flick through the sticky notes from the back of the pad to the front.

10 As you let the sticky notes go, the picture will appear to move.

These pictures show six stages. The more stages you put into a flip book the better. In your flip book, make the tongue only a tiny bit bigger each time.

Fabric Wall Hanging

Paint a design with PVA glue onto a piece of fabric to create a unique wall hanging for your bedroom.

You will need:

* 1 piece of white cotton fabric, 15cm x 40cm
* PVA glue with a pouring nozzle
* PVA glue with a spreader
* yellow acrylic paint
* water   * small paint pots or jars
* paintbrush
* green acrylic paint
* baking tin
* warm, soapy water
* kitchen towel
* 2 straight sticks, 4cm longer than the width of the fabric
* ruler
* 40cm length of string

To make this wall hanging you will need space to leave the fabric to dry for up to two days. Before you begin, check that the space is not needed for anything else.

1 Using the PVA glue with the pouring nozzle dribble glue onto the fabric in the shape of leaves. Add some decorative patterns. Leave the glue to dry.

2 Mix a squeeze of the yellow acrylic paint with the same amount of water in a small paint pot. Paint over some areas of the fabric and dried glue, as shown. Leave it to dry.

3 Mix a squeeze of the green acrylic paint with the same amount of water in another small paint pot. Paint over different areas of the fabric. Leave it to dry.

4 Soak the fabric in warm, soapy water in the baking tray or tin for 15 minutes. Carefully place the wet fabric onto a layer of kitchen towel. Peel off the glue. Leave the fabric to dry.

5 Place the fabric paint-side down. Spread glue along the edge of the top of the fabric. Fold the top 2cm over and press it down.

6 Repeat step 5 along the bottom edge of the fabric. Leave it to dry. Slide the sticks through the gaps you have created, top and bottom. Knot the string onto the top stick on either side of the wall hanging so that you can hang it up.

Snake Box

The snake design on this box is inspired by Aborigine paintings. Use the box to keep your precious possessions safe.

You will need:

* flat cardboard box
* blue paint
* paintbrushes
* thin white paper and pencil (for tracing the template)
* scissors
* fine point black felt-tip pen
* dark purple paint
* kitchen roll
* white paint
* yellow paint
* 2 stick-on jewels

1 Paint the box blue all over. Leave it to dry.

2 Use thin white paper and a pencil to trace the snake template on page 31. Cut it out.

3 Draw around the snake template on the box's lid with the black felt-tip pen. Remove the template.

If you like this style of painting, use library books or the Internet to research Aborigine paintings.

4 Paint the snake with dark purple paint. Leave it to dry.

5 Dip the hard end of the paintbrush into white paint. Make a dot 5mm from the edge of the snake. Make more dots, following the outline of the snake. Wipe the end of the paintbrush with kitchen roll and repeat, to create an outline of yellow dots, 2mm outside the first line.

If you are worried about the paint smudging, leave each row of dots to dry before you add the next.

6 Use the hard end of the paintbrush to create two more dotted outlines of the snake. Make more patterns all over the box with dots of paint until you are happy with the design. Decorate the snake's body with a yellow zigzag line.

7 Stick on jewel eyes.

Puffy Paint Picture

This paint works like magic. Watch your painting puff up in the microwave to create a great 3-D effect.

You will need:

* mixing bowl
* 6 tablespoons of self-raising flour
* 6 tablespoons of salt
* water
* three small mixing bowls or dishes
* brown ink or food colouring
* yellow ink or food colouring
* green ink or food colouring
* empty squeezy bottles (small washing up bottles or empty paint bottles)
* sheet of thick green paper or thin green card, 18cm x 18cm
* microwave oven

1 Measure the self-raising flour into the mixing bowl. Add the salt. Mix with water to make a smooth paste.

2 Divide the mixture into three small mixing bowls. Mix brown ink or food colouring into one bowl, yellow into another and green into the last one.

3 Pour the mixture into three squeezy bottles. Drizzle the yellow paint mixture onto the paper in the shape of a sunflower.

4 Add dots of brown mixture in the centre, to look like seeds.

5 Drizzle green mixture to make a stem and leaves to finish.

6 Ask an adult to microwave the picture for 30 seconds. The paint will puff up and harden.

Op Art Butterfly

This type of picture is based on geometric shapes. It has a real wow factor.

You will need:

* thin white paper and pencil (to trace the template)

* scissors

* fine point black felt-tip pen

* square of white card, 210mm x 210mm

* ruler * glue and spreader

* green, blue and purple felt-tip pens

* yellow, orange and red felt-tip pens

* thick black card, 250mm x 250mm

Op art stands for optical art, a style of painting made famous by artists such as Bridget Riley.

1 Use thin white paper and a pencil to trace the butterfly template on page 31. Cut it out. Use the black felt-tip pen to draw around it on the white card.

2 Using a ruler, draw lines in black felt-tip pen from the top to the bottom of the card. Angle some lines and vary the distance between them.

14

3 Colour in the background stripes. Keep switching colours between the orange, yellow and red felt-tip pens, as shown.

4 Colour in the stripes on the butterfly. Switch between purple, blue and green stripes, as shown.

5 Glue the back of the picture and stick it to the centre of the black card to frame it.

Try drawing around your hand instead of using the butterfly template.

Underwater Scene

Salt sprinkled on wet watercolour paint makes interesting patterns and textures – just right for an underwater scene.

You will need:

* watercolour paper
* blue and green watercolours
* paint palette
* paintbrush
* water
* salt
* magazines
* scissors
* feathers
* glue and spreader
* a party popper

1 Mix blue and green watercolour paint with water in a paint palette. Paint the watercolour paper blue and green.

2 Sprinkle salt onto the wet paint and leave everything to dry.

You can make your own watercolour paper by following the instructions on page 30.

3 Brush off the salt, to leave interesting patterns in the paint.

4 Cut fish shapes from magazines. Choose interesting patterns or colours. Glue the fish onto the picture.

5 Glue the feathers onto the bottom of the picture as seaweed.

Cut an uneven strip of paper from a magazine. Glue it along the bottom of the picture to look like the seabed.

6

7 Pop the party popper, remembering to point it away from people. Glue on some of the party popper strings to look like strands of seaweed.

Abstract Notepad

Make a plain notepad cover into a real work of art. This abstract style of painting was used by a famous painter called Mondrian.

1 Use the pen to draw around the bottom and sides of the notepad cover onto the black card. Join up the lines as shown in blue. Cut out the shape.

You will need:

* ballpoint pen
* notepad
* sheet of black card
* scissors
* masking tape
* paintbrush
* white acrylic paint
* yellow acrylic paint
* red acrylic paint
* double-sided sticky tape

Masking tape is easy to peel off the surface of the cover. Do not use sticky tape as it will tear the cover when you peel it off.

2 Tape strips of masking tape in horizontal and vertical lines onto the black card, as shown.

3 Painting over the masking tape, paint some of the areas of card in white, some in yellow and the rest in red. Leave to dry.

4 Carefully peel off the masking tape.

5 Fix double-sided sticky tape along each edge on the back of the card.

6 Remove the backing tape to fix the new notepad cover in place.
You can use this technique to decorate storage boxes and folders too.

19

Pop Art Poster

Print a simple self-portrait onto colourful paper squares and join them together to make a dramatic poster for your room.

You will need:

* styrofoam from a pizza base, 10cm x 10cm
* ballpoint pen
* scrap paper
* paintbrush
* white paint * black paint
* 4 squares of orange paper, 10cm x 10cm
* 4 squares of pink paper, 10cm x 10cm
* 4 squares of green paper, 10cm x 10cm
* kitchen paper
* masking tape
* sheet of stiff black paper, 34cm x 44cm
* PVA glue and spreader

1 Draw a simple self-portrait onto the styrofoam using a ballpoint pen. Press hard so that the lines are deep.

2 Paint a layer of white paint onto the styrofoam. Press it down onto scrap paper to get rid of any excess paint.

3 Press the foam printing block onto one of the orange paper squares. Lift it off and leave the print to dry.

4 Use the foam block to print onto one more orange, two pink and two green squares of paper.

5 Wash the white paint off the foam block under a running tap. Dry the styrofoam with kitchen paper. Paint the printing block with black paint. Use it to print onto two pink, two green and two orange squares of paper.

6 Leave to dry. Arrange the prints in a pattern, mixing up the colours and the black and white prints. Turn all the printed pictures face down.

7 Use masking tape to join all the squares into rows, as shown. Tape all the rows together. Glue everything onto black paper to finish your poster.

Bubble Painting

Have fun creating beautiful printed patterns with a bowl full of bubbles. Work quickly before the bubbles burst.

You will need:

* orange, purple and blue food colouring or ink
* teaspoon
* small bowl
* washing-up liquid * water
* dessertspoon
* plastic drinking straw
* A4 white paper
* A4 thin white card

If you are using ink, be very careful not to suck on the straw and swallow it.

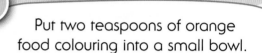

1 Put two teaspoons of orange food colouring into a small bowl.

2 Add a dessertspoon of washing-up liquid. Add two dessertspoons of water. Mix everything together with the spoon.

3 Use the straw to blow into the coloured liquid to make lots of bubbles.

4 Gently place a sheet of paper on top of the bubbles. Take a print of the orange bubbles.

5 Move the paper over, to take two more prints from the bubbles. Leave the paint to dry.

6 Repeat steps 1 – 3, using a clean bowl and blue food colouring. Place the sheet of paper with the orange bubble prints on top of the blue bubbles. Repeat steps 4 – 5. Leave to dry.

7 Repeat steps 1 – 3 using purple food colouring. Lay the sheet of paper with the orange and blue bubble prints on top of the bubbles. Take prints from the bubbles. Leave to dry.

8 You could repeat steps 1 – 7 using thin card. Fold the card in half and use it as a birthday card.

Heart Bunting

Practise some of the techniques used in this book and make a great room decoration at the same time.

Use thin white paper and a pencil to trace the heart template on page 31. Cut it out.

You will need:

* pencil and thin white paper (for tracing the template)

* scissors

* sheets of A4 white card

* string

* small pegs

AND

For the watercolour hearts:

* watercolour paints (blue, green, pink and purple)

* paintbrush

* water

* fine point felt-tip pen

For the dotted hearts:

* poster paints (blue, white, yellow and red)

* paintbrush

* felt-tip pen

Watercolour Hearts

1 Take one sheet of white card and paint some parts with blue watercolour paint and others with green watercolour paint. Wash the brush in clean water.

2 Blend the colours together using a clean wet paintbrush. Leave to dry.

3 Use the black felt-tip pen to draw around the heart template, as shown. Cut it out.

4 Repeat steps 1 – 3 using a fresh piece of white card and pink and purple watercolours to make a second heart.

Dotted Hearts

1 Use the template to cut a heart shape from white card. Paint it with blue poster paint and leave it to dry.

2 Dip the end of a felt-tip pen in white poster paint. Press it onto the heart. Repeat to make a line of dots that follows the outline of the heart.

3 Dip the end of a paintbrush in yellow paint to make a second line inside the first. You could complete your design by repeating the dotted heart shapes in the centre, as shown below. Make another heart with a yellow painted background.

This heart is cut out of bubble print paper. The instructions for this are on pages 22 – 23.

Peg the hearts onto the string. Tie the loose ends of the string to hang up the bunting.

Fireworks

The fireworks in this picture burst through the black paint as you scrape off the surface.

You will need:

* sheet of A4 thick white paper
* pink, green, red and yellow wax crayons
* newspaper
* black poster paint
* paintbrush
* sheet of A4 thin white paper
* coloured pencil
* paperclip, opened out

Try scratching off the paint with a lolly stick or a toothpick to get different effects.

1 Use the wax crayons to colour thick stripes of wax over the whole of a sheet of paper. Do not leave any bits of paper showing through.

2 Put the sheet of paper onto a layer of newspaper. Use poster paint to paint the paper black. Leave to dry. If the wax crayon is showing through, add a second layer of paint.

3 Sketch some exploding fireworks on the piece of thin white paper.

4 Copy the design onto the black paint with the coloured pencil.

5 Use the end of the opened out paperclip to scratch off the black paint, following the pencil lines. This will reveal the wax crayon colours underneath.

Try drawing thick circles of wax instead of stripes for a different effect.

Totem Pole

The rich bright colours of felt-tip pens make this totem pole very eye-catching.

You will need:

* cardboard tube from inside a kitchen roll
* piece of white paper the same height as the tube and wide enough to wrap around it with an overlap of 1cm
* pencil
* ruler
* fine point black felt-tip pen
* coloured felt-tip pens
* double-sided sticky tape
* scissors

1 Use a pencil to draw bird's eyes and a beak in the centre of the paper, 2cm from the top. Draw a second set of eyes and a beak 7cm from the bottom. Draw feet above the bottom set of eyes. Draw feathers over the rest of the paper, as shown below.

2 Go over the pencil lines with the black felt-tip pen.

A totem pole is a tree or carved wooden pole decorated with animals or symbols.

3 Use felt-tip pens to colour in the designs.

4 Turn the paper over. Put a strip of double-sided sticky tape down each side of the design. Peel the backing strip off one piece of tape and lay the tube onto it.

5 Peel the backing strip off the second piece of tape. Wrap your picture around the tube. Press it in place.

6 Use the template on page 32 to trace two pairs of wings. Cut them out.

7 Copy the wing design shown above or create one of your own. Go over the lines with black felt-tip pen. Use the felt-tip pens to colour in the pattern. Use a short strip of double-sided sticky tape to fix the wings to the back of the totem pole, as shown in the finished picture on the right.

Watercolour Paper

Make your own watercolour paper and use it to paint like a real watercolour artist. To make your own watercolour paper you wet paper that is taped to a board. It will wrinkle at first but once it has dried it will not wrinkle again when you paint on it.

1 Tape all the sides of the paper to the pastry board, as shown, and press it down firmly with your fingers.

You will need:

* masking tape
* A4 cartridge paper
* clean pastry board or chopping board
* paintbrush
* water

2 Use the paintbrush to brush a layer of water over the paper. It will wrinkle. Leave it to dry – it will flatten as it dries. Carefully remove the masking tape. Now you have a sheet of watercolour paper.

Templates

Op Art Butterfly
Pages 14 – 15

Heart Bunting
Pages 24 – 25

Snake Box
Pages 10 – 11

31

Frog Flip Book
Pages 6 – 7

Totem Pole
Pages 28 – 29

Index

Further Information

Websites

Explore art and artists by visiting the websites of the National Gallery, Tate Modern and Tate Britain. Each website has dedicated areas for children.

Books

Art Treasury by Rosie Dickins (Usborne) An introduction to famous artists and artworks with simple projects based on the techniques they used.